Marine Force Recon
in Action

SPECIAL OPS

by Michael Sandler

Consultant: Fred Pushies
U.S. SOF Adviser

BEARPORT
PUBLISHING

New York, New York

Credits

Cover and Title Page, © Hans Halberstadt dba Military Stock Photography; 4, © Shawn Baldwin/The New York Times/Redux; 5, © Shawn Baldwin/The New York Times/Redux; 6, © Fred Pushies; 7, © Fred Pushies; 8, © LCPL R. R. Bazinet, USMC 6TH Marine Regiment; 9, © LCPL Nicholas J. Riddle, USMC; 10, © Courtesy of Jim Vesterman; 11, © Hans Halberstadt dba Military Stock Photography; 12, © Cpl. Mike Escobar; 13, © LCPL Ryan LeDoux, USMC; 14, © Bettmann/CORBIS; 15, © Michael S. Yamashita/CORBIS; 16, © George Gellatly/NFL/Getty Images; 17, © National Archives; 18, © Photo Courtesy of SUNY Cortland; 19, © Department of Defense Photo (USMC); 20, © U.S. Marine Corps photo by Lance Cpl. Kelly R. Chase; 21, © U.S. Navy photo by Journalist 2nd Class (SW) Brian P. Biller; 22, © Scott Peterson/Getty Images; 23, © AP Photo/The Daily News/Don Bryan; 24, © Shawn Baldwin/The New York Times/Redux; 25, © REUTERS/HO/Cpl. Paul Leicht; 26, © AP Images/Jacksonville Daily News, Chuck Beckley; 27, © Fred Pushies; 28A, © Fred Pushies; 28B, © Fred Pushies; 28C, © Fred Pushies; 29A, © Fred Pushies; 29B, © Fred Pushies; 29C, © Fred Pushies; 29D, © Garmin Ltd.

Publisher: Kenn Goin
Senior Editor: Lisa Wiseman
Creative Director: Spencer Brinker
Design: Debrah Kaiser
Photo Researcher: Jennifer Bright

Library of Congress Cataloging-in-Publication Data

Sandler, Michael, 1965–
  Marine Force Recon in action / by Michael Sandler ; consultant, Fred Pushies.
      p. cm. — (Special ops)
  Includes bibliographical references and index.
  ISBN-13: 978-1-59716-634-8 (library binding)
  ISBN-10: 1-59716-634-0 (library binding)
  1. United States. Marine Corps—Juvenile literature. 2. Special forces (Military science)—United States—Juvenile literature. 3. Scouting (Reconnaissance)—United States—Juvenile literature. I. Title.

  VE23.S25 2008
  359.9'64130973—dc22

                                    2007040744

For more information, write to Bearport Publishing Company, Inc., 101 Fifth Avenue, Suite 6R, New York, New York 10003. Printed in the United States of America.

10 9 8 7 6 5 4 3 2

Contents

At War in Iraq

U.S Marines were headed for Fallujah. **Rebels** had taken over the Iraqi city. The Americans had to force them out.

A few special men, known as Force Recon Marines, had already sneaked inside the town. Captain Jason Schauble led them through Fallujah's dark streets. Bullets flew at the Marines. **Grenades** exploded nearby.

A U.S. soldier outside of Fallujah runs for cover during fighting.

They were in great danger. Jason's men, however, kept moving. Without them, the U.S. attack might fail.

U.S. Marines fire at the enemy in Fallujah.

The United States went to war in Iraq in March 2003. The Battle for Fallujah began in November 2004.

Force Recon Marines

Like all Force Recon Marines, Jason Schauble was trained for a special job—**reconnaissance**, or recon for short. Recon means finding out information about the enemy. Where are their soldiers? Where do they keep their weapons? What are the best ways to fight them?

A Recon Marine uses binoculars to help spot the enemy.

Answering questions like these helps armies win battles. No one helps answer these questions better than Recon Marines.

Along with the Army, Navy, and Air Force, the Marines are part of the U.S. **military**.

Recon Marines use special equipment to help find enemy locations.

In Action

Force Recon Marines take many risks to learn about the enemy. They travel deep behind **enemy lines**.

Sometimes they arrive by boat, other times by helicopter or **parachute**. They are always careful not to be discovered.

Force Recon Marines are trained to jump from planes flying as high as 25,000 feet (7,620 m).

This Recon Marine slides down a rope from a helicopter.

Recon Marines move quickly and silently. They climb mountains. They swim across rivers. They **scuba dive** beneath the sea. Every **mission** is different. Recon Marines do whatever it takes to finish a job. They are the Marines' most highly skilled fighters.

Recon Marines wear clothing and face paint to help blend into their surroundings so they are not easily seen.

Recon School

Marine Jim Vesterman was exhausted. He had barely slept in a week. Every muscle in his body screamed in pain. Things were about to get worse, however. His instructor was asking him and his team to run five miles (8 km)—carrying a telephone pole!

Jim Vesterman

Not everyone can go to Recon School. You have to be male, in the Marines, and pass a hard **physical** test.

The exercise was part of Recon School. Here, Marines learn recon skills such as **patrolling**. They also learn how to be tough soldiers. How hard is it? More than a third of all **trainees** drop out the first week.

A trainee stops to do push-ups during a 5-mile (8-km) march. Trainees carry 35-pound (16-kg) backpacks.

More Training

Recon School is only the beginning. Force Recon Marines go through two full years of training.

After Jim passed Recon School, he moved on to jump school, where he learned how to parachute. Next he went to dive school, where he became an **expert** scuba diver.

A Recon Marine gets ready for parachute training.

Jim's final course was escape school. He was taught what to do if he was caught by the enemy.

Which was the most important skill Jim learned during training? Teamwork! Force Recon Marines must count on one another for survival!

Jim finished training in 2003. The following year, he served in Iraq with the 3rd Force Reconnaissance Company.

Recon Marines during scuba dive training

World War II

Recon Marines got their start during World War II (1939–1945), when America was fighting Japan. One of their most important missions came in July 1944.

America was ready to attack the Japanese at Tinian, an island in the Pacific Ocean that had many beaches. U.S. military leaders had to choose which beach their soldiers should land on. If a beach was well **defended** by the enemy, many Americans could die!

U.S. warplanes fly over Tinian after bombing Japanese planes.

Two Marine Recon teams were given these orders:
*Go to Tinian. See which beaches are safest. Make it
back alive!*

One of Tinian's many beaches

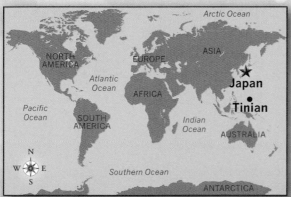

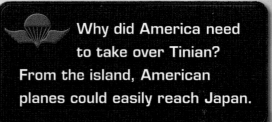

Why did America need
to take over Tinian?
From the island, American
planes could easily reach Japan.

Into the Water

Jim Martin, Olie Kelson, and Don Neff were three of the Recon Marines sent to check out the beaches. They boarded a U.S. **destroyer** headed for Tinian.

The big ship stopped before getting too close. The Marines then got into a small rubber raft. They glided through the dark Pacific Ocean.

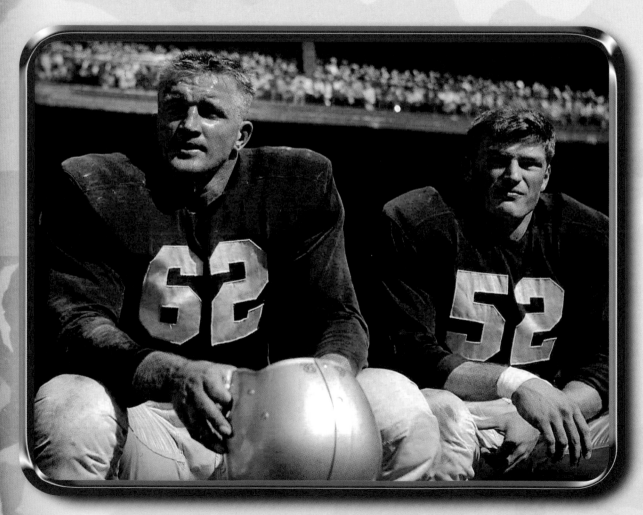

After the war, Jim Martin (#62) became a star football player.

Near Tinian, the Marines jumped out. They swam silently toward shore.

If spotted, they'd be shot. Luckily, clouds covered the moon. The darkness hid the swimmers.

U.S. Marines headed for Tinian.

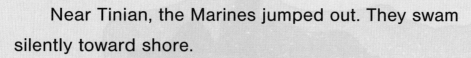
The three Marines were swimming to Yellow Beach. It was one of the top choices for the attack on Tinian.

Yellow Beach

Soon, the three Marines crawled up onto the beach. Japanese guards shone lights down at the water. Luckily, they didn't see the Americans.

Lieutenant Don Neff was awarded a Silver Star for his bravery at Tinian.

The Marines explored carefully. Don climbed through **barbed wire**. He moved dangerously close to Japanese soldiers. He was so close that he could hear them talking.

All three kept track of what they saw—mines, boulders, steep cliffs, and guns. A Yellow Beach landing would be a disaster! Finally, the Marines jumped back into the sea and returned to the destroyer.

The Marines told officials what they learned on their mission. Due to this information, a different beach was used for the attack. Thousands of lives were saved.

The Recon Marines saw guns like this one on Yellow Beach.

Recon Teams

Today, Force Recon Marines work in teams of four-to-six men. Missions can last up to one week. During the day, the Marines usually rest. They do their work at night.

At Tinian, Recon Marines entered the water with nothing but knives. Today's Marines carry lots of gear. Night vision goggles let them see in the dark. Telescopes give views of faraway enemy camps. Radios send information instantly.

A Marine may carry over 100 pounds (45 kg) of gear in his backpack.

Force Recon Marines also carry rifles and pistols. If discovered, they must be ready to fight.

Teamwork is very important to Recon Marines.

Force Recon Marines don't just do recon. Since they are such skilled fighters, they also go on special **combat** missions.

Into Fallujah

During missions, Force Recon Marines are glad they are well trained. Jason Schauble's men needed all their skills inside Fallujah. As soon as they entered the city, Iraqi rebels started firing at them.

U.S. Marines patrolling the streets of Fallujah

More than half of Jason's 24 men were injured in Fallujah.

Bullets flew down from rooftops. Jason and his men kept **scouting**. Then they took safety inside an **abandoned** home.

Once inside, they **radioed** officers waiting outside of town. They told them what they had learned about the city and the rebels.

Staff Sergeant Mark Detrick was one of the Recon Marines working with Jason Schauble. Here he is receiving a Purple Heart.

Victory

Soon the Battle for Fallujah began. The information found by Jason and his team helped the U.S. **commanders**. They knew the best roads to drive their tanks into the city. They knew where the rebels were hiding. They knew where to have planes drop bombs.

U.S. Marines were able to take over this
bridge used by the enemy in Fallujah.

As American troops stormed into town, Recon
Marines kept working. They fired on rebels who attacked
U.S. soldiers.

Soon the rebels were on the run. Marine Force
Recon helped drive them out of Fallujah.

The Battle for Fallujah was
called Operation Phantom
Fury by the U.S. military.

A U.S. Marine jet, loaded with
bombs, flies near Fallujah.

An Easy Choice

A few months later, Jason led his team on a farmhouse **raid** in Iraq. Rebels began shooting. One Marine was shot and fell to the floor. As the Marines took cover outside, Jason went back in for his teammate. The rebels opened fire again.

Jason was shot three times, but stayed inside. He led the attack as his men took control of the house.

Jason was awarded a Silver Star and a Bronze Star for his bravery. However, due to his wounds, Jason had to leave **active duty**.

For Jason, the choice to go back in had been simple. For Force Recon Marines, the team always comes first.

Force Recon Marines

Force Recon Marine Gear

Force Recon Marines use lots of equipment to carry out their missions. Here is some of the gear they use.

Rubber rafts take Marines on recon missions.

Battery-powered **radios** send messages back to base.

A **digital camera** allows Marines to photograph enemy targets.

The **M4-A1 Carbine** is one of the weapons Marines use in combat.

Radio headsets help Marines talk to one another during missions.

GPS devices tell Marines exactly where they are going.

Night vision scopes let Force Recon Marines see in the dark.

Glossary

abandoned (uh-BAN-duhnd) empty, no longer used

active duty (AK-tiv DOO-tee) when soldiers are ready to go into battle

barbed wire (BARBD WIRE) wire with small, sharp points, used for fences

combat (KOM-bat) fighting

commanders (kuh-MAND-erz) leaders of a group of soldiers

defended (di-FEND-id) protected

destroyer (di-STROI-ur) a fast warship

enemy lines (EN-uh-mee LINEZ) areas of land from where the enemy fights

expert (EK-spurt) when a person is very skilled at something

grenades (gruh-NADEZ) small bombs that are thrown by hand

military (MIL-uh-*ter*-ee) having to do with armies or war

mission (MISH-uhn) a special job

parachute (PAH-ruh-*shoot*) a soft cloth attached to ropes that is used to slow down one's fall after jumping out of a plane or helicopter

patrolling (puh-TROHL-ing) watching or walking around an area to protect it

physical (FIZ-uh-kuhl) having to do with the body

radioed (RAY-dee-ohd) sent a message using a radio device

raid (RAYD) a quick, surprise attack

rebels (REB-uhlz) soldiers who are fighting against a government

reconnaissance (rih-KAH-nuh-zinss) the gathering of information about an enemy

scouting (SKOUT-ing) moving around to gather information

scuba dive (SKOO-buh DIVE) deep underwater diving using special breathing equipment; *scuba* stands for Self-Contained Underwater Breathing Apparatus

trainees (trane-EEZ) people who are learning how to do something by practicing

Bibliography

Lanning, Michael Lee, and Ray William Stubbe. *Inside Force Recon: Recon Marines in Vietnam*. New York: Ballantine (1989).

McDonnell, Patrick J. "Marines of Force Recon Set the Stage in Fallouja." *Los Angeles Times* (December 6, 2004).

Pushies, Fred J. *Marine Force Recon*. St. Paul, MN: MBI Publishing (2003).

Shaw, Henry I., Bernard C. Nalty, and Edwin T. Turnbladh. *Central Pacific Drive: History of U.S. Marine Corps Operations in World War II* (Vol. III). USMC Historical Branch (1966).

Time. "Crusaders & Slaves," Vol. XLVIII, No. 16 (October 14, 1946).

Vesterman, Jim. "From Wharton to War," *Fortune Magazine*, Vol. 153, No. 11 (June 1, 2006).

Read More

Hamilton, John. *The Marine Corps (Defending the Nation)*. Edina, MN: Checkerboard Books (2007).

Voeller, Edward. *U.S. Marine Corps Special Forces: Recon Marines*. Mankato, MN: Capstone Press (2000).

Learn More Online

To learn more about Force Recon Marines, visit
www.bearportpublishing.com/SpecialOps

Index

About the Author

Michael Sandler has written many books for children and young adults. He lives in Brooklyn, New York, with fellow writer Sunita Apte and their two children, Laszlo and Asha.